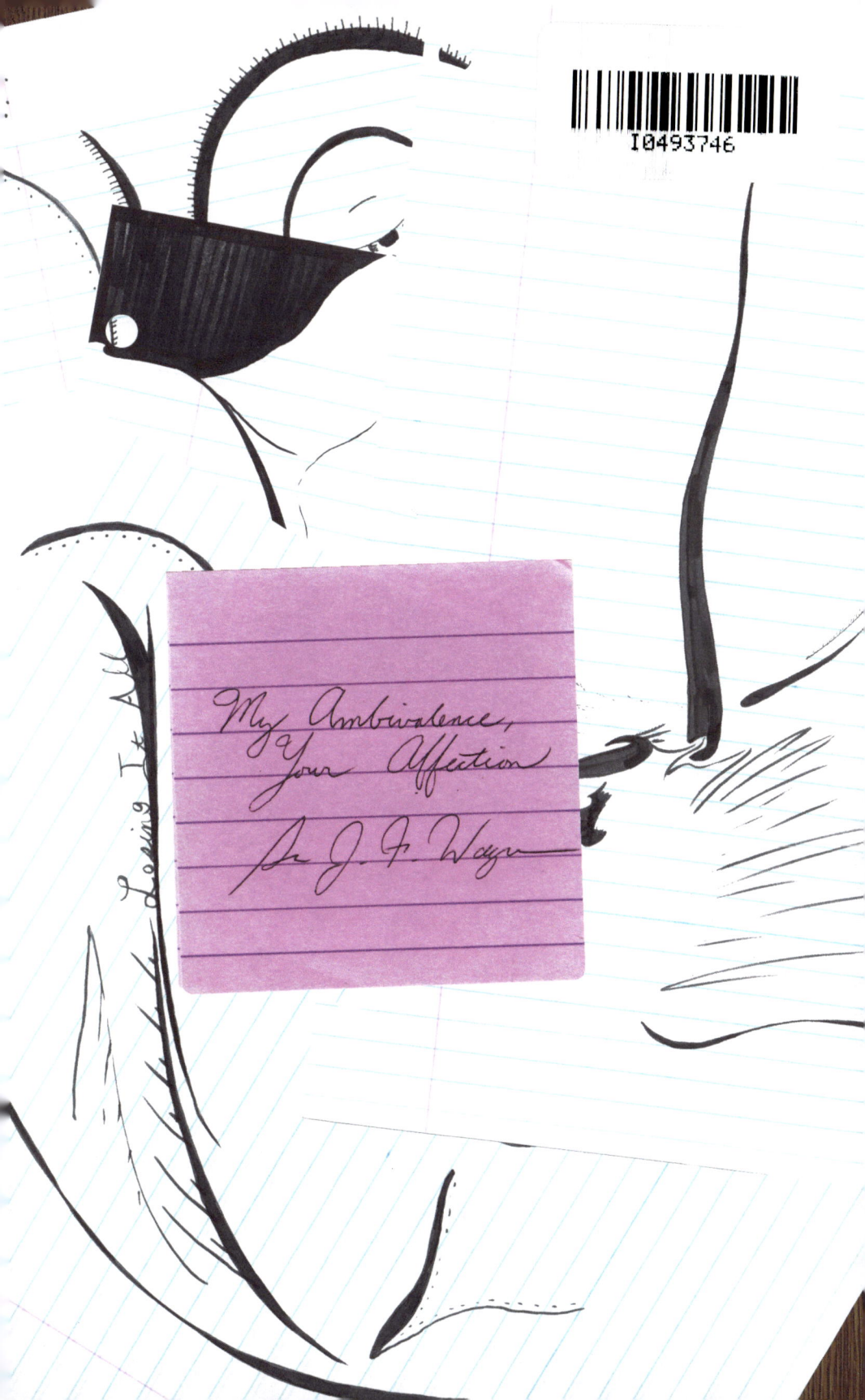

ISBN-10:0989735540
ISBN-13:978-0-9897355-4-4

My Ambivalence, Your Affection is something that's been percolating in my mind for a few years. In 2011, between *Testimony* and *Loveless*, I planned on releasing a short portfolio of drawings. Long story short, I didn't feel confident enough to actually publish those particular drawings. (They sucked…) Fast forward to now, a short four months since *Waiting*, and I'm releasing this portfolio of recent drawings and writings. I feel they have their place in my artistic practice and hold more intimate value than my watercolors; they are certainly more spontaneous and much more honest than anything you'll find in my paintings. Due to the nature of the writings in this collection I want this to be clear: I'm not releasing this to put anybody on the spot or to get back at anybody. I was incredibly hesitant to include any of the notebook pages in this collection because of the context in which they were originally created. Everything included here, drawings and writings, are included because of their value to each other as art pieces. I don't consider this a "story" book. In some ways, I suppose it could be considered non-sequitur. In the end, it's up to the reader to determine what it is or if this collection holds any value to anyone but me.

This collection is dedicated to the women that I have the privilege of calling my friends. How you gals put up with me, I'll never know, but your patience, understanding, and friendship are some of the greatest treasures in my life.

Ian J.F. Wagner
Dec. 2013

What words can I
write that even conceive
of her beauty?
   All I can say, is
that whenever I'm near
her, everything is alright.
   I just want to hold
her, so tightly. But...

                    I wonder
                how she
             really feels...

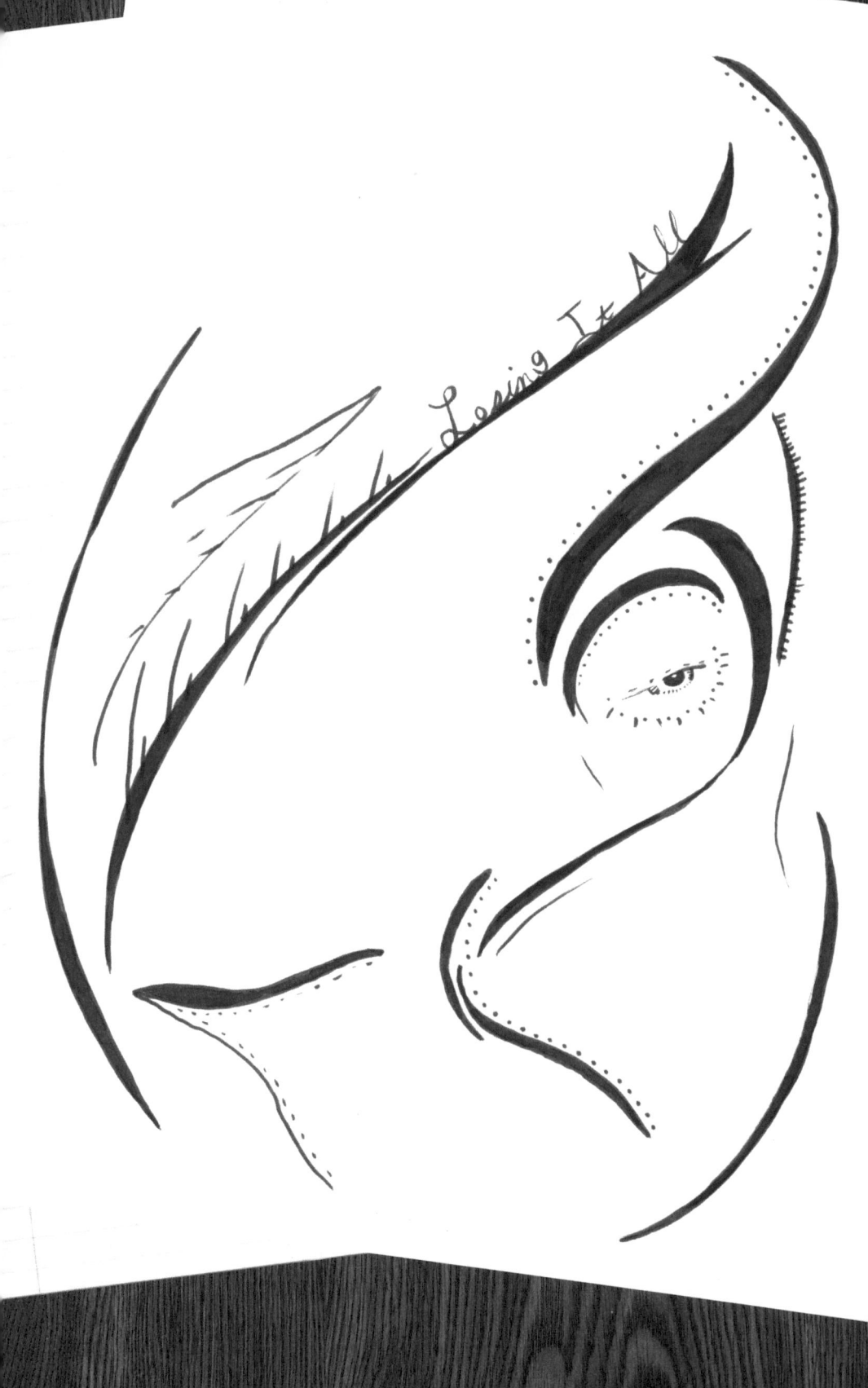

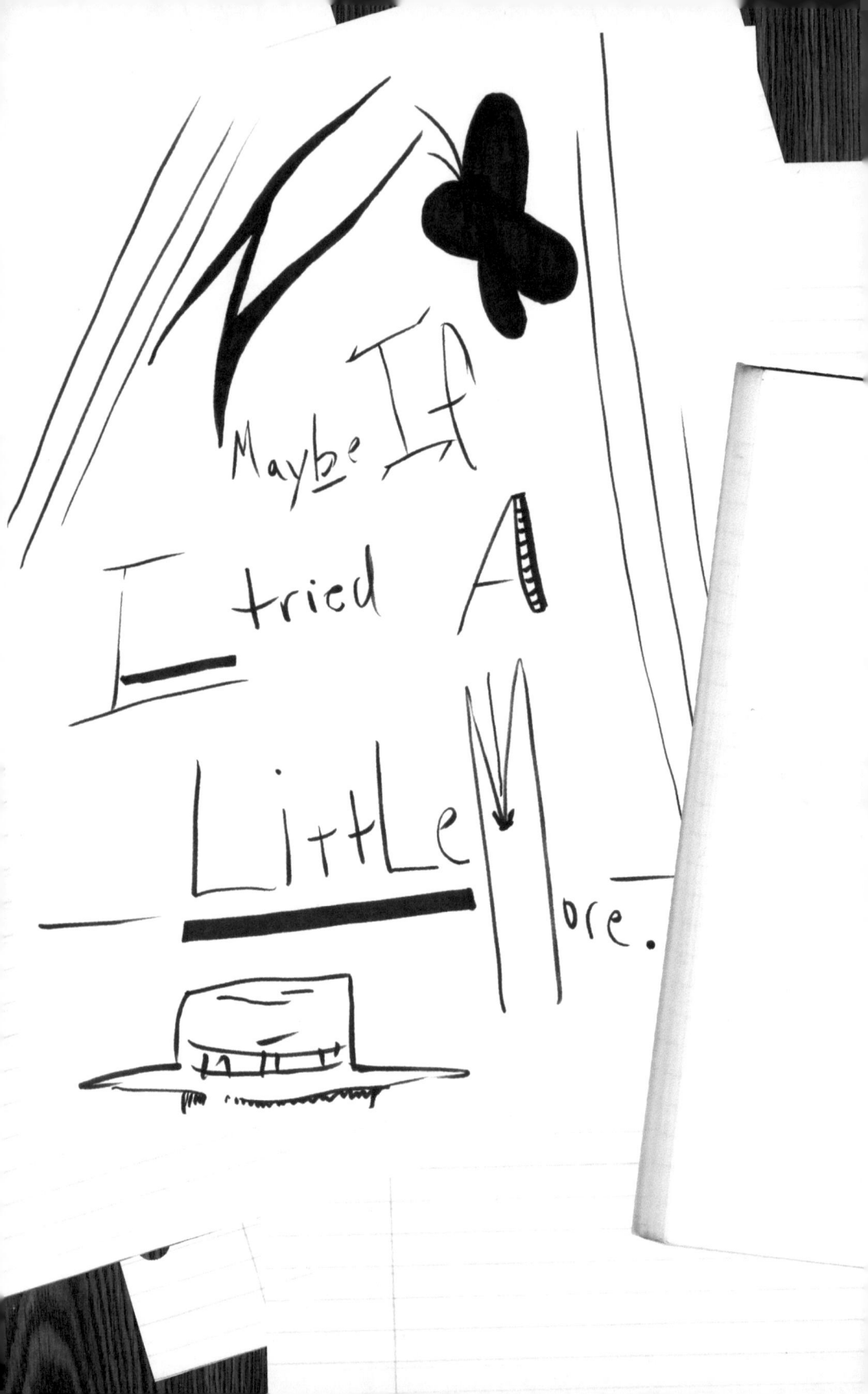

Why does it feel like I've jumped the gun whenever I'm positive? Every single fucking time... It feels fantastic to be optimistic, but I need to reel it in a bit and maintain some realist perspective. I need to evaluate whether this thing is worth pursuing any further. I think I jumped the gun on that too. Do I give up? Do I keep trying? Is it really worth it? I don't have it in me to say "yes" right now. I can't say "no," either. Or is it that I don't want to admit the answer is "no"?

I should just let it shatter.

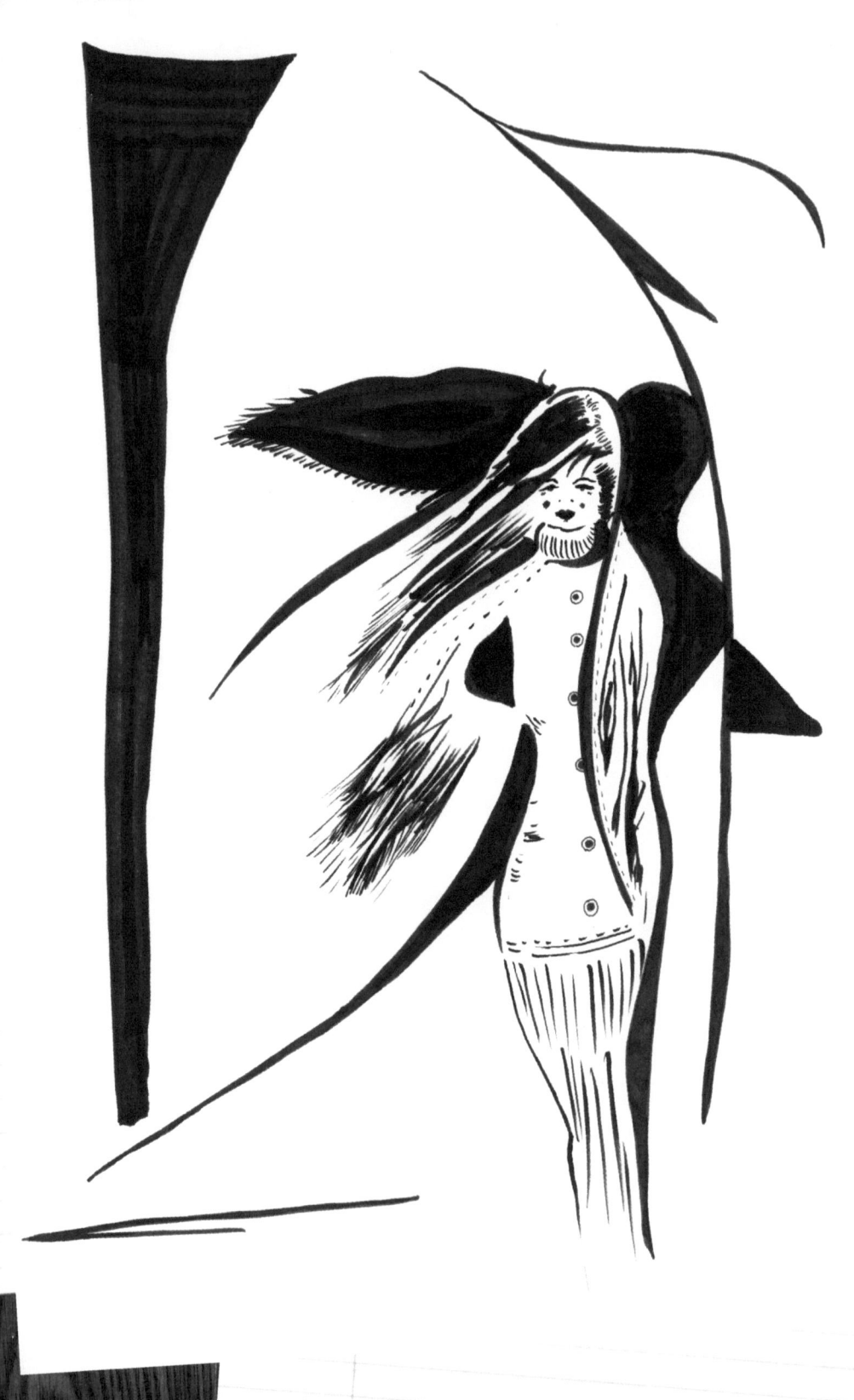

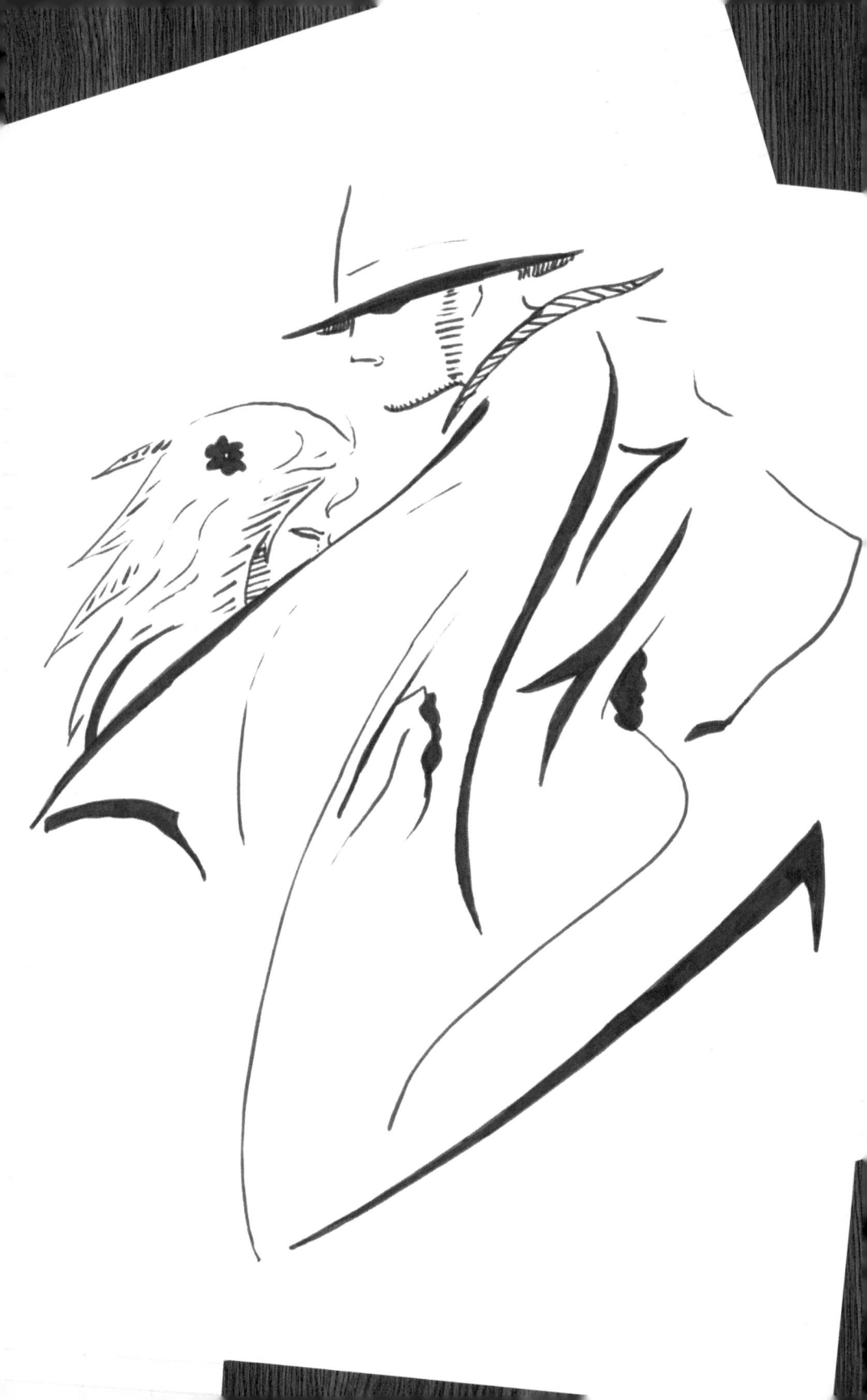

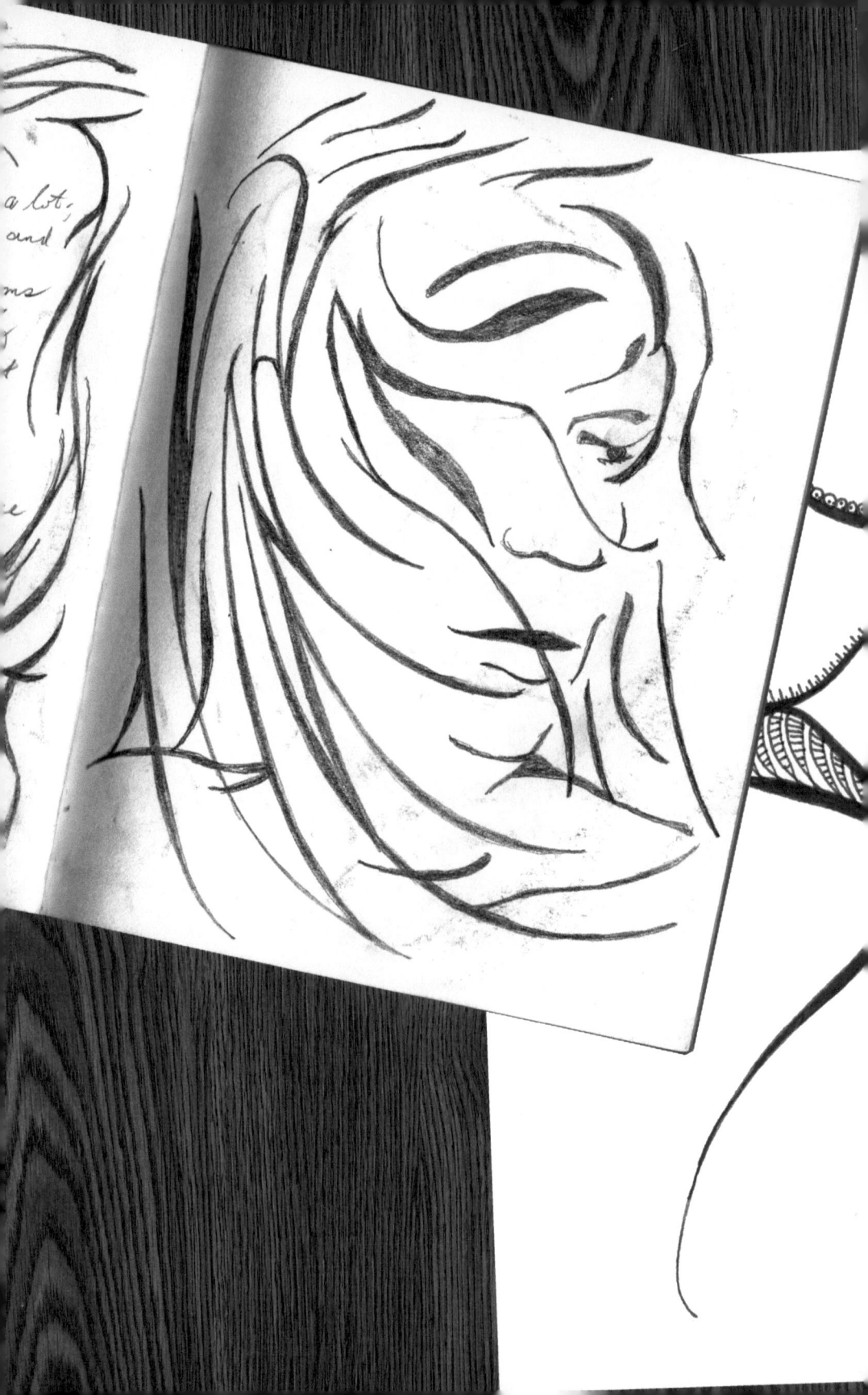

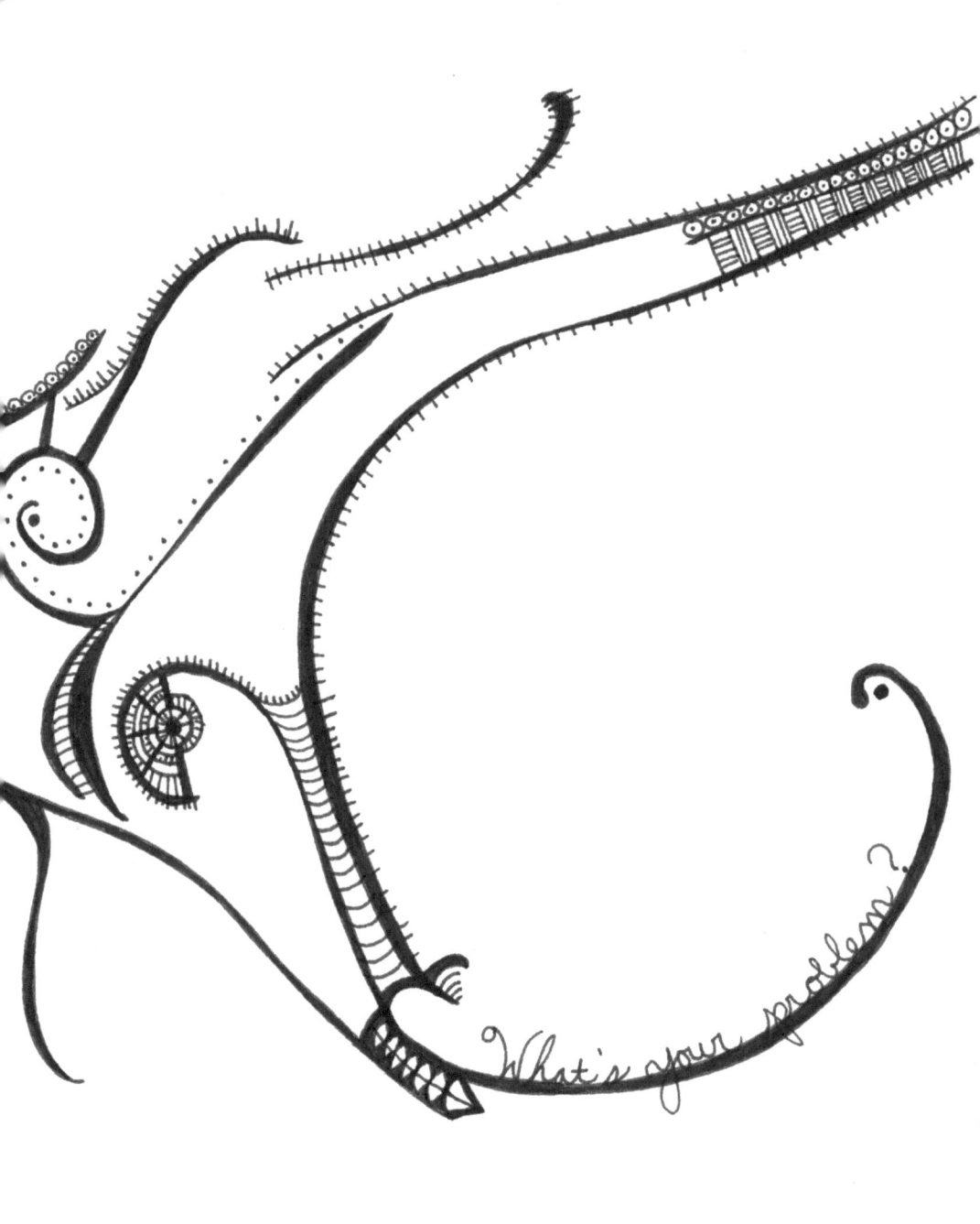

What's your problem?

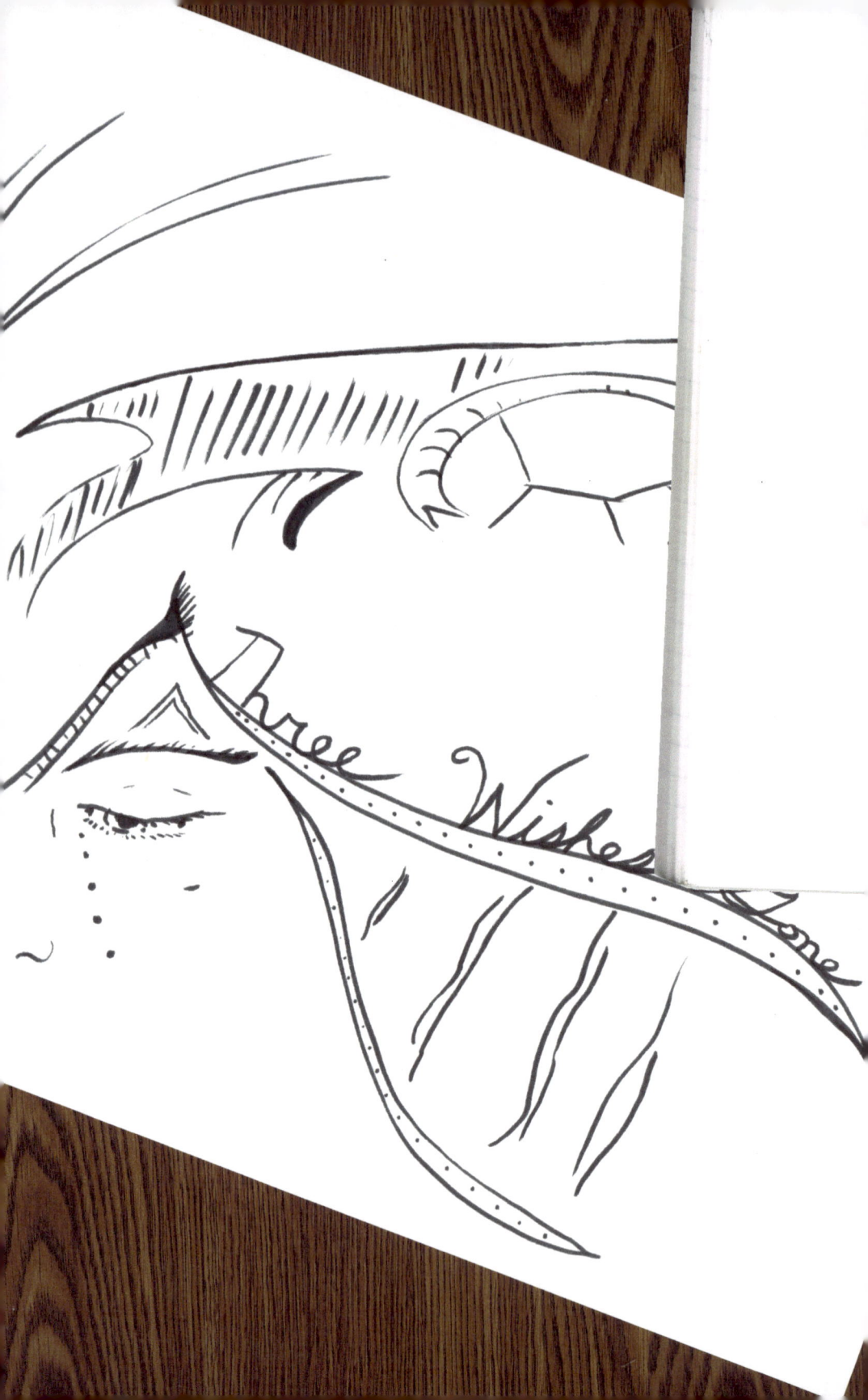

What
am
I
thinking?
I don't know...
what
are
thinking? you

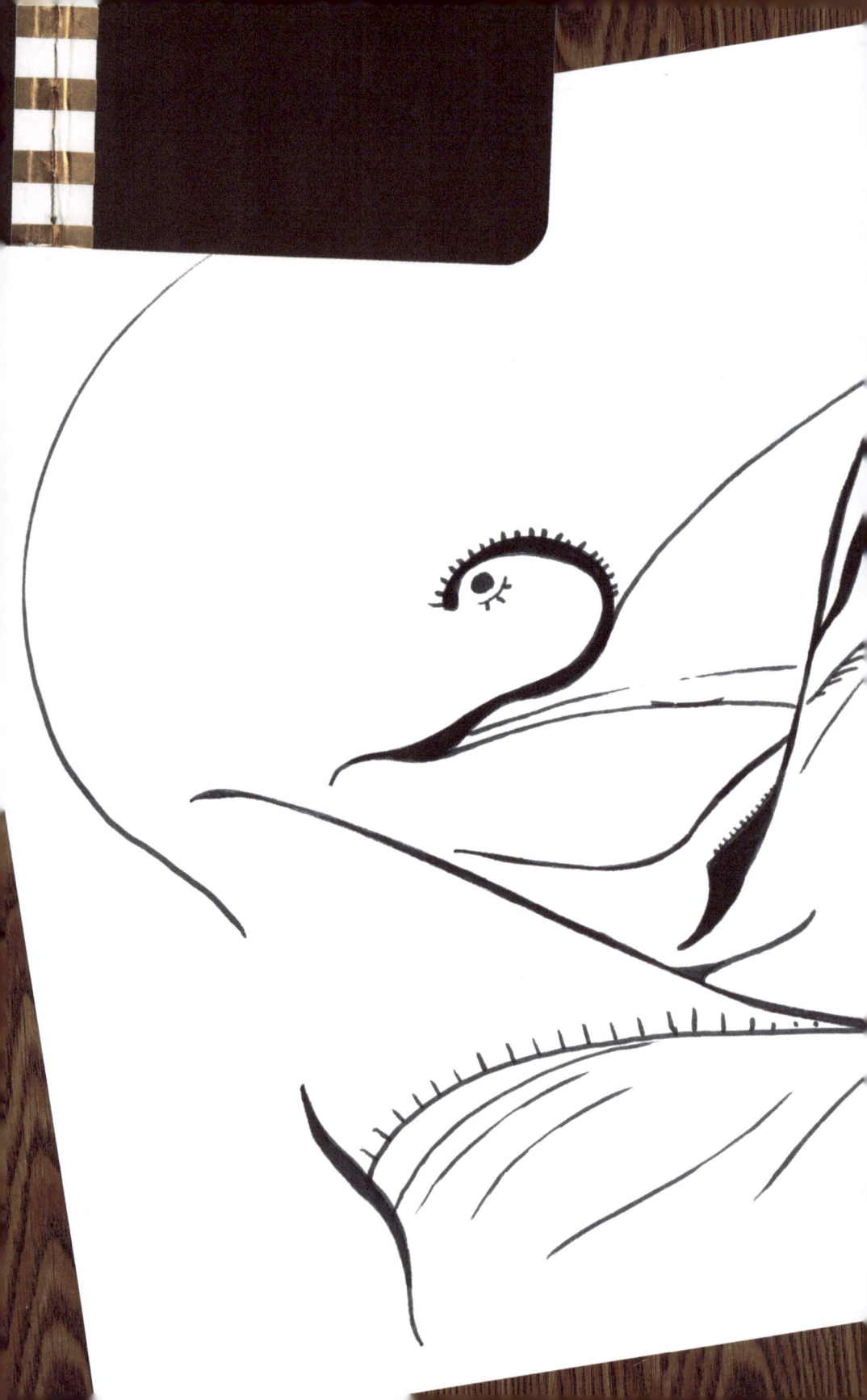

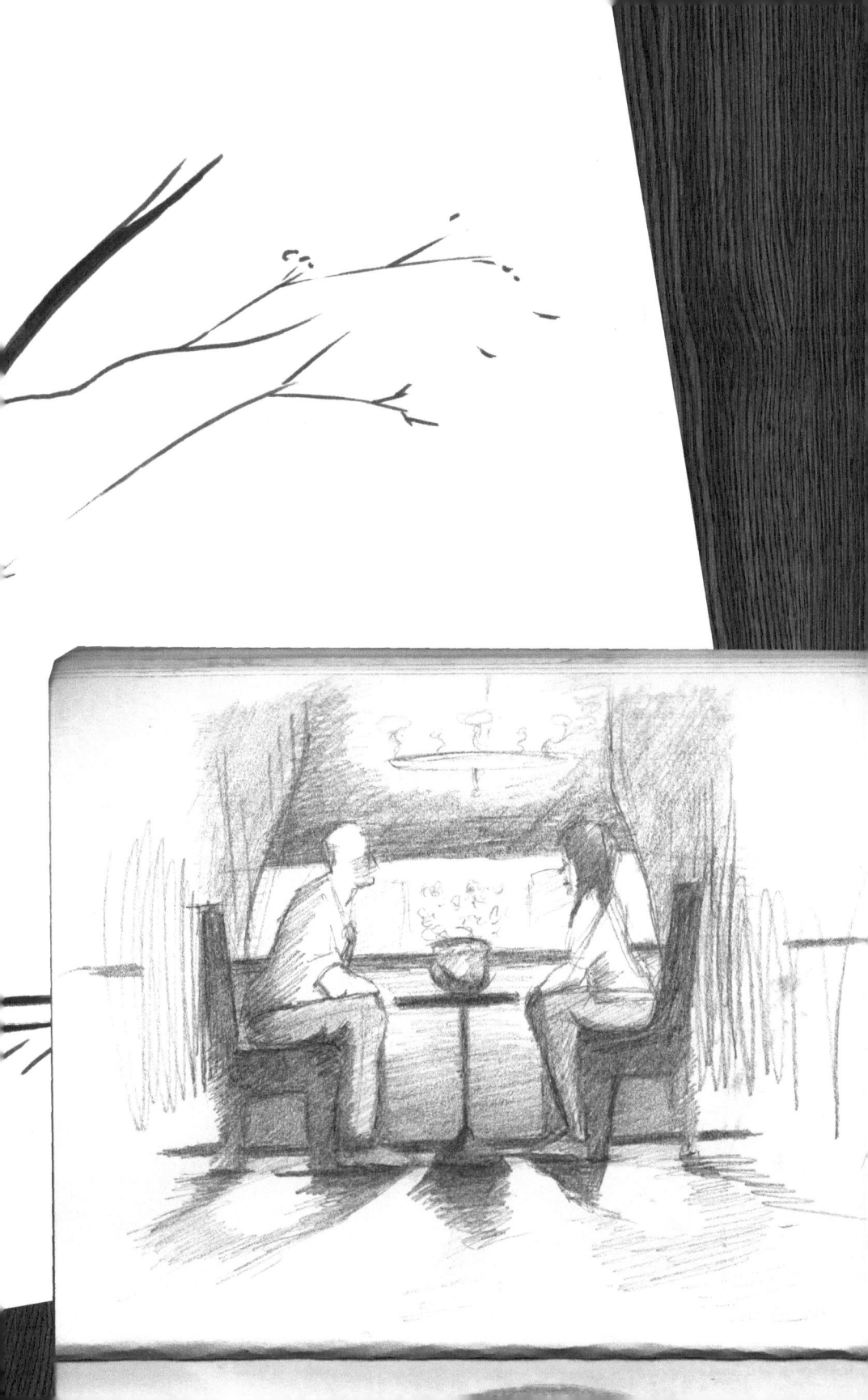

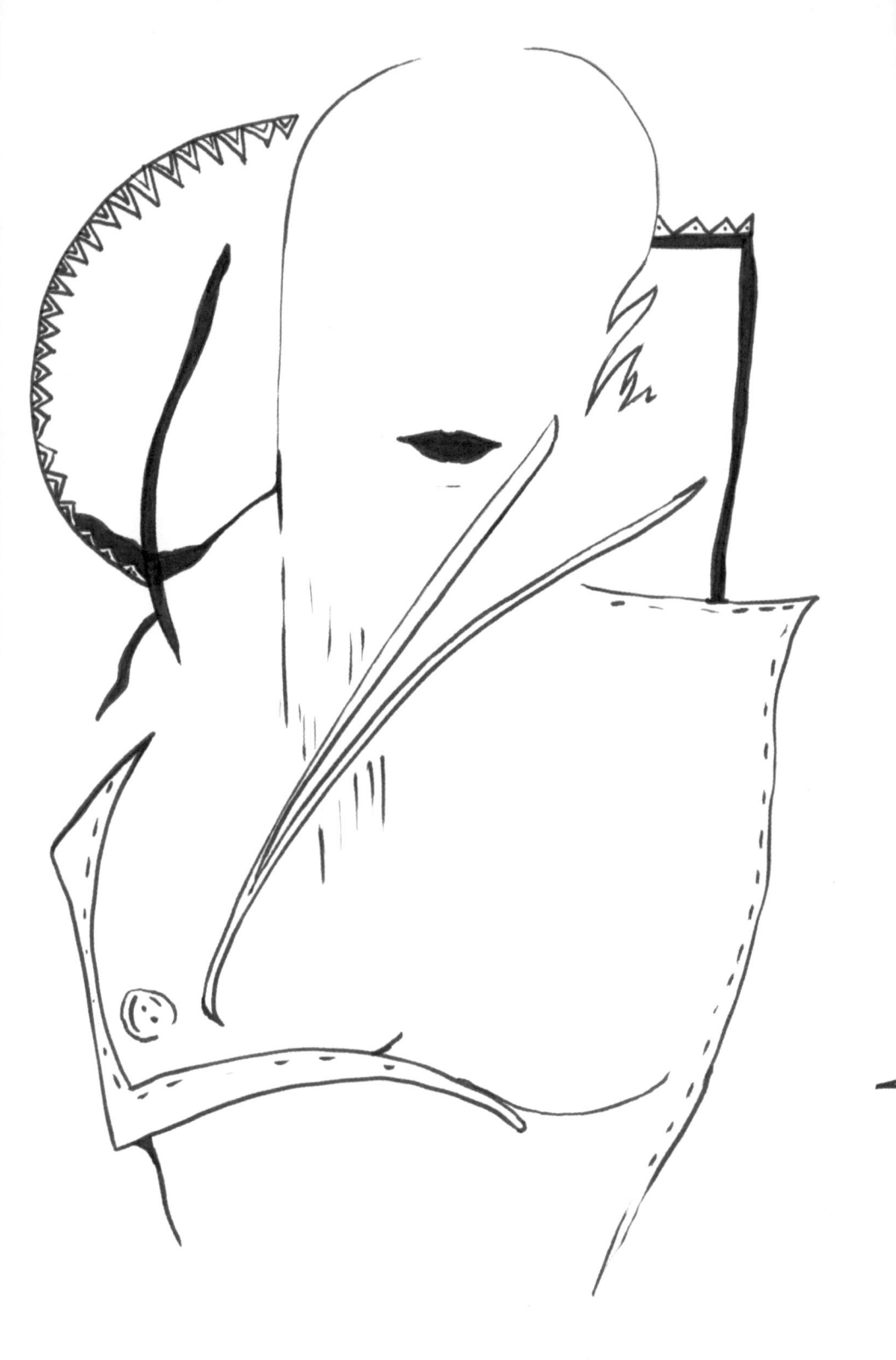

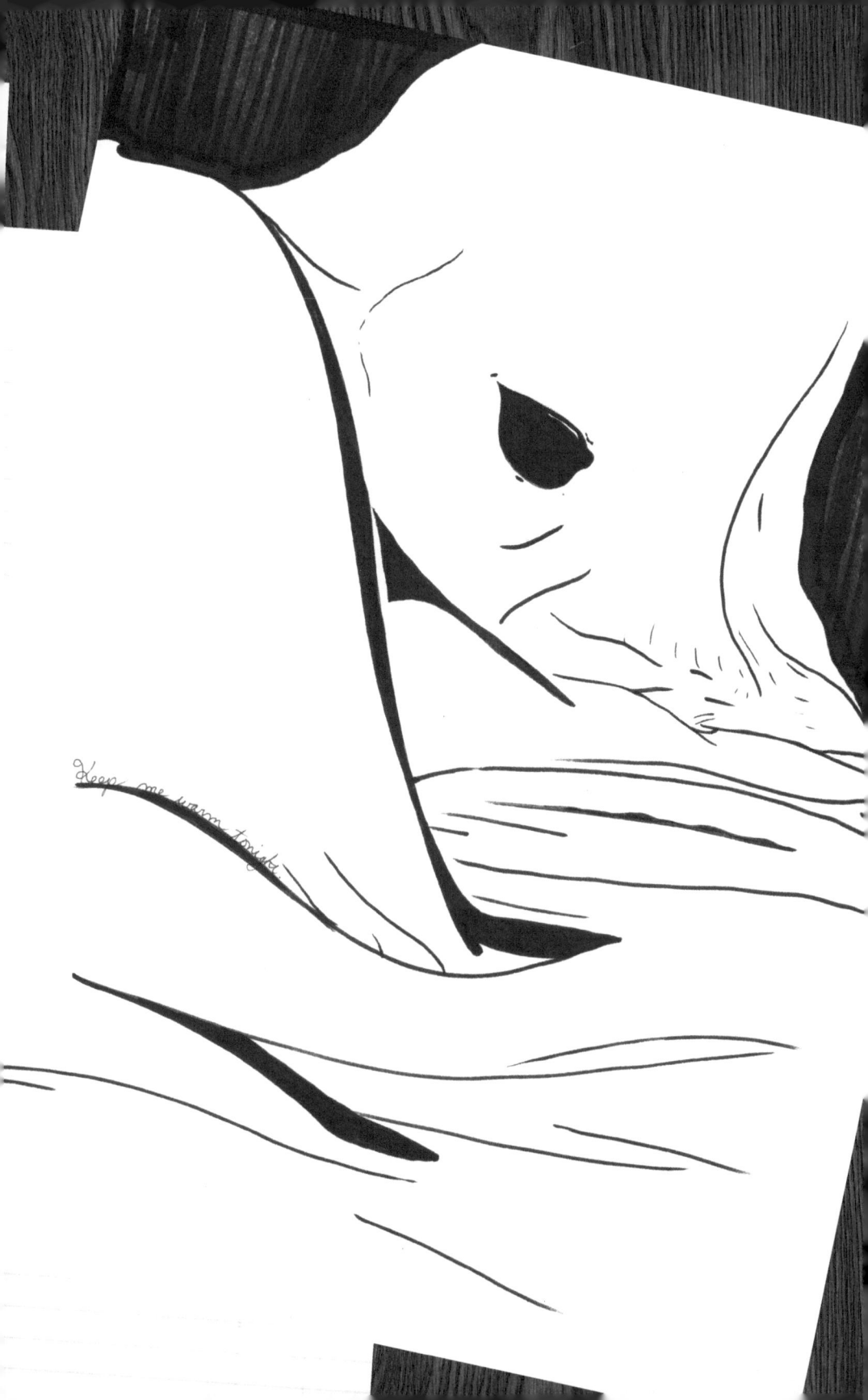

The little things mean
so much more...
so much more...

I hope she'll
keep me around.

Is her
assessment
of my situation correct?
I don't know if
it is love...
or if I want it
to be...

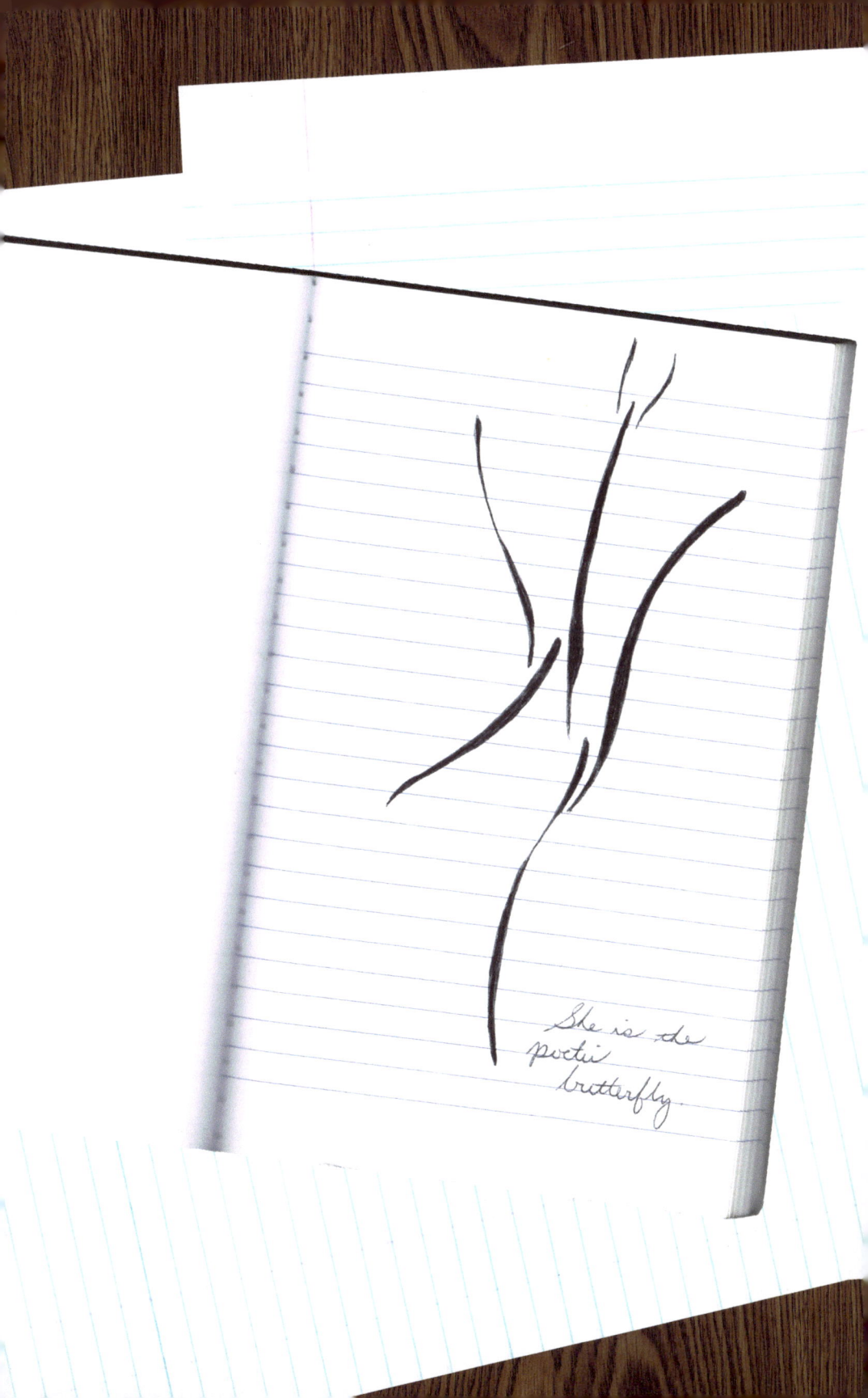

She is the
poetic
butterfly.

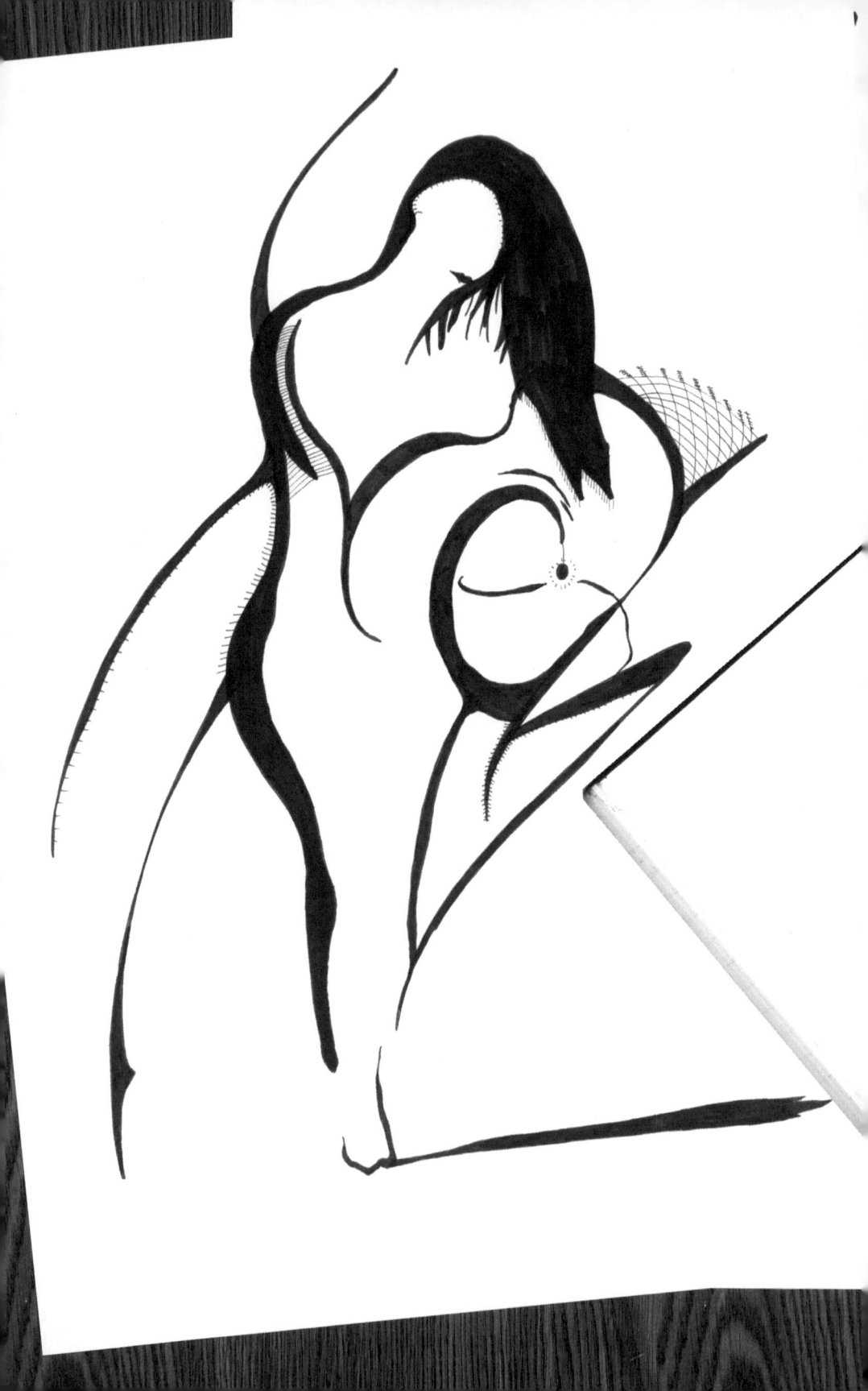

Don't look at me like that.

There is no second guessing. It's as clear that it's come to this, but it is the best for both of us. Everything is clear to me now.

I've come to the right decision.

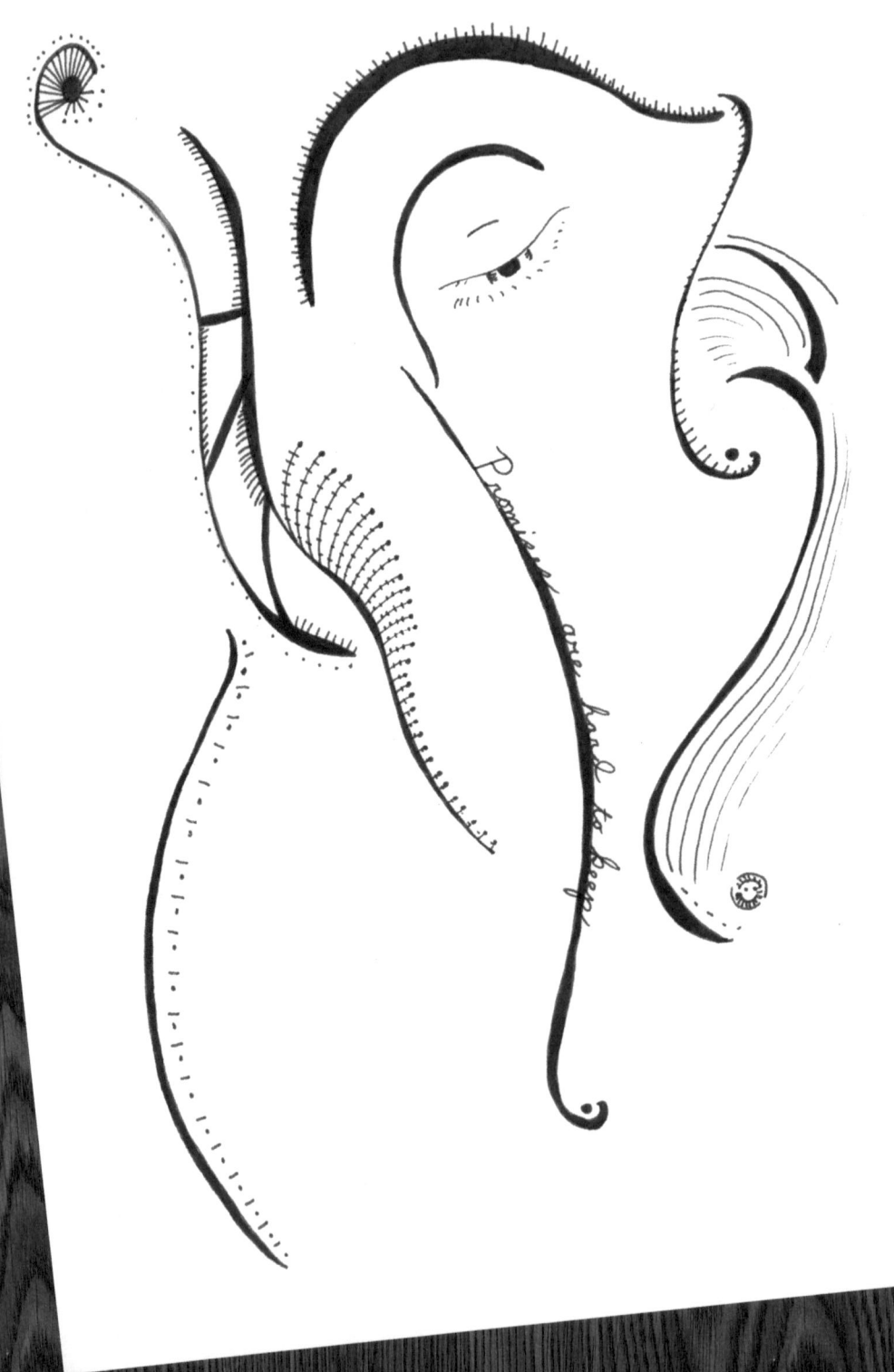

It's getting harder
and harder to forget.
This time last year
I couldn't wait to
see. Now, I'm dreading
the thought of seeing
again.

It'll never be
the same, but
I'll see what
happens.

I don't
miss
it
anymore.

Satisfaction is the death of desire